# Where to Find Minibeasts

# Minibeasts Under a Stone

## Sarah Ridley

A+

## Smart Apple Media

Smart Apple Media
P.O. Box 3263, Mankato, Minnesota 56002

Printed in the United States

Published by arrangement with the Watts
Publishing Group Ltd, London.

Library of Congress Cataloging-in-Publication Data

Ridley, Sarah, 1963-
    Minibeasts under a stone / Sarah Ridley.
        p. cm. -- (Where to find minibeasts)
    Includes index.
    Summary: "Profiles many insects and
invertebrates found under stones, discussing their
eating habits, habitats, and survival skills"--Provided
by publisher.
    ISBN 978-1-59920-326-3 (hardcover)
    1.  Soil invertebrates--Juvenile literature.  I. Title.
    QL365.34.R53 2010
    592'.1757--dc22

                                                      2008044909

Series editor: Sarah Peutrill
Art director: Jonathan Hair
Design: Jane Hawkins
Illustrations: John Alston
With thanks to our models: Zhané Edgar and
Finlaye Johnson

**The measurements for the minibeasts in this book are typical sizes for the type of species shown in the photographs. Species within groups can vary enormously in size.**

9 8 7 6 5 4 3 2 1

# Contents

Words in **bold** are in the glossary on pages 28–29.

# Under a Stone

Carefully lift up a stone and you may discover a hidden world of minibeasts underneath. Stones create a safe, dark **habitat**, perfect for many minibeasts.

▲ Several types of minibeasts shelter under stones or build their homes there.

## TOP TIP!

When you are hunting for minibeasts under stones, always replace the stones carefully. If you have taken a minibeast away to study it, return it close to the stone and it will find its own way home.

## What Is a Minibeast?

Minibeast is the name given to thousands of small animals, from bees to butterflies, worms to woodlice, and snails to spiders. Although many are **insects**, others are not. None of them have a **backbone** so scientists give them the name **invertebrate**.

## Minibeasts Under a Stone

The minibeasts that you are most likely to find under a stone are: woodlice, ants, beetles, earwigs, centipedes, slugs, and snails. Use the identification guide on pages 26–27 to identify these minibeasts, and a few others that you might find as well.

▲ Centipedes (right) eat woodlice (left) so this woodlouse had better watch out!

## Safe Hideout

Stones provide many minibeasts with somewhere safe to hide from **predators**. Several of the minibeasts in this book are the favorite food of bigger animals such as toads, frogs, birds, mice, hedgehogs, and badgers.

◄ A thrush smashes snails' shells against a stone to get to the soft bodies inside.

# Sheltering Snails

Snails can be hard to find in the daytime. Many of them shelter from the sun under rocks and stones. Here, the coolness and the dampness stop them from drying out.

◀ Two snails leave their stone shelter. Snails often return to rest in the same spot.

This snail shell is ¾ inch (1.8 cm) long.

## The Shell

The snail's hard shell protects it from enemies because the snail can pull itself right inside. The shell also helps to stop the snail from drying out. In very hot or cold weather, the snail pulls itself inside its shell and seals the entrance with slime.

Snails have two pairs of **tentacles** on their heads. The longer pair has a small black dot at the end—the snail's eyes.

# Watch it Eat!

**What you will need:**
- A snail   • A jar
- A vegetable (lettuce leaf, cabbage, etc)
- A magnifying glass

**What to do:**
- Collect a snail and put it in a jam jar with some vegetable leaves.

- Use your magnifying glass to watch how the snail scrapes away at a leaf. It uses rows of tiny teeth, called radula, on its tongue.

- Remember to put the snail back where you found it.

## TOP TIP!

You could also search for snails under plant pots or logs and amongst ivy and other trailing plants.

# Slimy Slugs

Slugs are like snails without a shell. Because of this, they are even more likely to dry out, so they shelter under stones to stay alive.

This slug can grow almost 6 inches (15 cm) long.

▲ Slugs, like snails, are **mollusks**, but they move faster than snails.

▶ If it feels it is in danger, a slug will curl up small.

## All that Slime

Slugs have tiny **glands** all over their skin that make a thick slime. This stops slugs from drying out and helps them to move along on their flat "foot"—the part of the body that is in contact with the ground.

### TOP TIP!

Slugs love warm, wet weather so you are most likely to see them in spring and fall. Also, look for slugs in clumps of plants, in piles of leaves, under pots, or in compost heaps.

## Love Them or Hate Them

Slugs have many enemies. Birds, hedgehogs, frogs, toads, foxes, and beetles all love to eat them. Gardeners often hate slugs and try to kill them because they eat so many plants. Although slugs are destructive, they also help us all by eating dead and decaying plants.

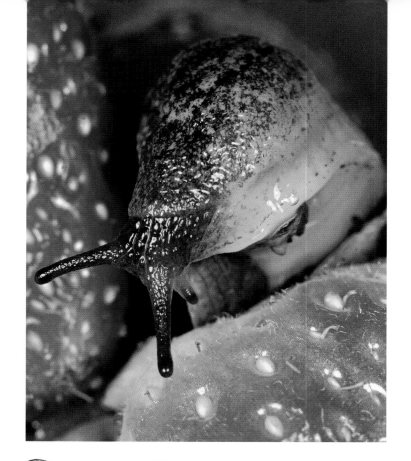

▲ Slugs can cause a lot of damage to fruit, vegetables, and other plants.

## TOP TIP!

Slugs and snails make slime to create a slippery track to help them move along. Look out for dried-up slime trails. They might lead you back to a resting slug or snail under a stone.

# Woodlice Homes

Lift up a stone and you may see small grey animals running for darkness. These are woodlice. They love the cool, damp habitat under a stone.

◀ Woodlice are **crustaceans** and they have 14 legs.

This woodlouse is ¾ inch (1.8 cm) long.

## TOP TIP!

Woodlice like living in other damp, dark places. Carefully lift pieces of wood or plant pots to see if they are there. They also live under the bark of trees, in walls, and in compost heaps.

## Woodlouse Armor

Look closely at a woodlouse and you will notice how the body is covered in what looks like armor. This tough covering protects the soft body inside. In order to grow, the woodlouse has to shed its hard skin for a bigger size that it grows underneath.

▲ A woodlouse sheds its skin in two stages. This one has already shed the back end and is now shedding the front.

This pill woodlouse is ⅜ inch (1 cm) long.

## Lovely Trash

Woodlice like to eat dead or rotting plants. They help clean up our gardens by feeding on dead plants, leaves, fallen trees, fungi, or compost. They are **nocturnal** like many of the minibeasts in this book.

◀ The pill woodlouse, also called the pill bug, can roll itself into a ball if scared.

# Earwigs—Good Mothers

Earwigs like the dark, damp habitat under stones or in cracks in sidewalks. They are nocturnal.

Earwigs got their name because people believed that earwigs crawled inside your ear and laid their eggs. Although they could do so, they don't—so there is nothing to worry about!

This earwig is ½ inch (1.3 cm) long.

## Night Feeders

At night, earwigs come out to feed on dead plants and animals. However, they also eat some live insects, such as **aphids**.

▶ Although they are nocturnal, you may find earwigs on flowering plants in the daytime. They like to eat plant **nectar**.

14

# Parenting

Unlike many insects, the mother earwig cares for her young. She lays her eggs under stones or in the soil in the autumn. Then she stays with the eggs all winter. When the tiny, pale earwigs, called **nymphs**, hatch in the spring, the mother earwig stays with them for another two weeks.

▲ The mother earwig cleans and protects her eggs.

▼ A male earwig's **pincers** are bigger and more rounded than a female's.

## TOP TIP!

Look further for earwigs in rotting leaves, under logs, under the bark of trees and in hollow plant stems.

Female

Male

# How to Look at Minibeasts

Most minibeasts are easy to damage unless we take care. Here's how to watch them without hurting them.

**What you will need:**
- Small boxes, jars, or plastic containers with lids
- A fine paintbrush or blade of grass
- A magnifying glass

**What to do:**
- Prepare some dry containers.
- Find some minibeasts under a stone. Move each minibeast gently using the paintbrush or grass.
- Be patient and let the minibeast do most of the moving.
- Keep different types of minibeasts in separate containers.
- Use a magnifying glass to take a closer look.
- If you put a lid on the container, make small air holes so the minibeast can breathe.
- Use the identification guide on pages 26–27 to identify your minibeasts.
- Return the minibeasts close to where you found them.

# Minibeast Motel

The minibeasts in this book can all be found living under stones, rocks, or plant pots. You could try to attract some of these minibeasts to a minibeast motel.

## What you will need:
- Small boxes, jars, or plastic containers with lids
- Half a melon or grapefruit
- A knife  • A spoon  • Adult help

## What to do:
- Ask an adult to help you cut a melon or grapefruit in half and scoop out the inside. Cut "doors" in both sides of the skin to allow minibeasts to enter.
- Place the fruit in a shady spot overnight.
- In the morning, check to see if any minibeasts are visiting.
- After a few days, throw the fruit in the compost heap or trash, removing any minibeasts first.

▶ A slug might make the minibeast motel its home for a day or two.

# Ant World

Lift up a stone and you may find an entire ants' nest underneath. The stone provides a safe, warm, and dry place for the ants to build their nest and raise their young.

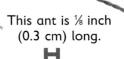

This ant is ⅛ inch (0.3 cm) long.

▲ You are most likely to find black ants like this. If you find red ants, beware—they bite and it hurts.

## The Nest

Ants build nests, also called colonies, under stones, under the ground, or in mounds. A stone helps to protect the entrance to the colony. An ants' nest is made up of many passageways connected to hollowed-out areas, called chambers. The queen ant lives in one of the chambers, laying eggs. Other chambers contain eggs, **larvae**, or **pupae**.

queen

◀ If the nest is disturbed, the ants hurry over to move eggs, larvae, and the queen to safety.

# Worker Ants

Most of the ants in the nest are worker ants. Each has a job to do. Some spend their time moving soil to build new areas of the nest, or to repair it. Others care for the eggs, larvae, and pupae. Many go outside to hunt for food to feed the colony.

▲ This top layer of an ants' nest shows the eggs and larvae in chambers connected by passageways.

◀ Worker ants feed the larvae, which look like maggots or tiny legless caterpillars.

# Hungry Ants

Ants hunt caterpillars, flies, aphids and **grubs** for food. They also like to eat the nectar made by plants, as well as **honeydew**—the sweet liquid that aphids make.

## Follow the Scent Path

When an ant finds some food and cannot carry it back to the nest, it returns to the nest, leaving a scent trail behind it. It passes the message to other worker ants that there is some good food along its scent pathway. The worker ants run back and forth along the scent pathway, collecting the food.

▲ An ant captures a woodlouse. Ants can carry things that are 10, 20, or even 50 times heavier than themselves.

# Ant Watching

To watch worker ants go about their jobs, you could try the following experiment.

## You will need:

• Jam or sweet food

• A spoon

## What to do:

• Find an ant in a garden. If you can't see one, follow these instructions anyway and see whether any come along.

• Place a bit of jam or some sweet fruit in front of the ant and watch what happens next.

• You should see the ant pick up some of the food and head off to the nest. Can you see where that is?

• Hopefully the ant will return with some other ants and continue feeding.

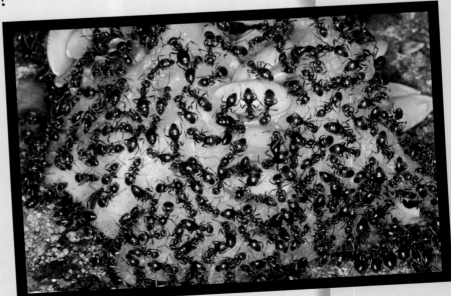

▶ Lots of ants have found this melon.

21

# Beetles and Centipedes

You will have to be quick to see centipedes and beetles that rest under stones. They are fast runners and will set off as soon as they are disturbed.

## Fast Beetles

Ground beetles and rove beetles leave their stone shelters at night to scurry about catching food. They have strong, long legs that help them to run fast. They hunt other minibeasts, including slugs and small insects.

This beetle is ½ inch (1.4 cm) long.

▲ Ground beetles have strong jaws for killing and crunching up their **prey**, such as this young slug.

◄ Many beetles, like this ground beetle, have long **antennas,** like thin threads, sticking out from their heads. These help them to smell prey and feel their way in the dark.

This beetle is ⅝ inch (1.5 cm) long.

# Speedy Centipedes

While many centipedes live in soil, some types shelter under stones. Other minibeasts fear these fierce, fast nocturnal hunters. Centipedes speed along on legs that stick out on both sides, feeling their way with their antennas. When they catch their prey, they inject poison into it.

This centipede is 1 inch (3 cm) long.

▲ Centipedes hunt and eat all sorts of minibeasts, including beetles, slugs, woodlice, and each other!

## TOP TIP!

Look for centipedes under logs, plant pots, or in the soil. A longer, paler type of centipede lives in the soil.

# Making a Pitfall Trap

A pitfall trap can help you to catch minibeasts.

**What you will need:**
- A jar or plastic container
- A spade or shovel
- Four small stones
- A big, flat stone, bathroom tile, or piece of plastic wrap.

**What to do:**
- Dig a hole big enough for your jam jar or container.

- Sink the container into the hole, so the rim is level with the soil.

- Place a piece of plastic wrap or similar flat object on four stones around the container, forming a roof with a gap underneath it so that the minibeasts can fall in the trap. This will stop any rain from drowning the minibeasts.

- Leave the trap overnight and check it in the morning.

## TOP TIP!

The identification guide on pages 26–27 will help you to identify the minibeasts.

- After you have identified your captives, release the minibeasts. Remember to check the trap every morning, or your minibeasts will die of hunger or eat each other!

- Remove the container and fill in the hole when you have finished.

▼ This pitfall trap has a specially built plastic cover. You can simply prop a piece of clear plastic on small stones.

# Identification Guide

Use this guide to help you identify the minibeasts that you find. They are listed in the order in which they are featured in the book. There are thousands of different minibeasts, so you may need to use a field guide or the Internet, too.

**Snail**: The snail carries its shell on its soft body and is a mollusk like the slug.

**Ant**: The ant is an insect and is related to wasps and bees. There are thousands of different types of ants worldwide. They live in nests, also called colonies.

**Slug**: A mollusk, the slug has a shiny, wet body and moves along on its one "foot." The slug's tentacles help it to see, feel and smell.

**Beetle**: An insect with two pairs of wings. The front wings are a hard, shiny wing case to protect the soft back wings, used for flying.

**Woodlouse**: A small, usually grey minibeast with a hard, armored skin. It is a crustacean and lives in dark, damp places.

**Centipede**: A fast-moving, flat, long minibeast. It has one pair of legs on each section of its body. It can be found under stones, in cracks, or in soil.

**Earwig**: A small, brown, shiny insect with pincers at the back of its body. It usually lives under stones or in cracks in walls or the ground.

Here are some other common minibeasts you might come across. Some are mentioned in this book.

**Millipede**: The millipede is long and slim but is more tube-shaped, rather than flat like the centipede. It moves along smoothly on its many legs.

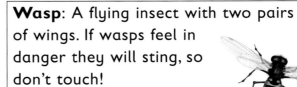

**Aphid**: A small green or black insect that belongs to the bug family. Like all bugs, it has a sharp, piercing mouth. It feeds by sucking on plants.

**Mite**: This tiny animal has eight legs and is an arachnid, like the spider.

**Bee**: Bees are flying insects and there are many types. Some live in nests with other bees while others live alone. All bees sting if they feel they are in danger, so don't touch!

**Silverfish**: Silverfish have remained almost the same since the time of the dinosaurs. These small, grey insects like dark, damp places and feed on tiny plants in the soil.

**Beetle grub**: The young of a beetle, also called a larva. Some grubs live underground; others live in rotting wood.

**Spider**: Spiders come in all shapes and sizes but they all have eight legs and a body in two parts. They belong to the arachnids and are not insects.

**Ladybug**: A flying insect with two pairs of wings. Ladybugs are small beetles that eat aphids.

**Wasp**: A flying insect with two pairs of wings. If wasps feel in danger they will sting, so don't touch!

**Harvestman**: A harvestman has eight legs and a body in one piece. It belongs to the **arachnid** family of animals, like the spider.

**Worm**: This long pink or red animal lives under the ground.

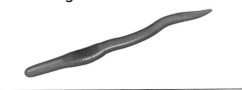

# Glossary

**Antennas** Feelers on an insect's head, used for smell, taste, and touch.

**Aphid** A small insect that belongs to the bug family.

**Arachnid** An animal with eight legs, like a spider, harvestman, or mite.

**Backbone** The line of bones down the middle of the skeleton.

**Crustaceans** A large group of animals, usually with a hard skin or shell and including woodlice, crabs, and lobsters.

**Gland** In slugs, a tiny body part that produces slime.

**Grub** The larva of certain beetles and other insects.

**Habitat** A place where plants and animals live.

**Honeydew** A sweet liquid made by an aphid, squeezed out of its bottom, and collected by ants to feed to their young.

**Insects** A huge group of animals. All insects have a body in three parts: the head, the thorax in the middle, and the abdomen at the end. Six legs are attached to the body and many insects have two pairs of wings.

**Invertebrate** A huge group of animals that don't have backbones, including insects, worms, and spiders.

**Larva (*plural,* larvae)** The stage in the life cycle of many insects after they hatch from eggs.

**Mollusks** A large group of animals with soft bodies. Slugs, snails, octopuses, mussels, and oysters are all mollusks.

**Nectar** The sweet liquid made by flowers and eaten by many insects.

**Nocturnal** Animals that rest during the day and are active at night.

**Nymph** A type of larva (see left).

**Pincer** A claw used to grab things.

**Predators** Animals that hunt other animals for food, rather than eating plants.

**Prey** An animal hunted or caught for food.

**Pupa (*plural, pupae*)** Part of the life cycle of many insects before they turn into adults.

**Tentacle** On a snail or slug, a springy thread on the head, used to help the animal feel or see its way around.

# Web Sites to Visit

**www.kiddyhouse.com/Snails**
A site with a lot of information on snails.

**www.oum.ox.ac.uk/thezone/index.htm**
The Oxford University Museum of Natural History web site has an Instant ID site to help you identify minibeasts.

# Index